Love and Codependency

How To Improve Communication and Love Yourself In A Codependent Relationship

Table Of Contents:

Chapter 1: Defining Co-dependency in Relationships

Chapter 2: Recognizing Co-dependency: Quizzes, Symptoms and Characteristics for the Co-dependent

Chapter 3: Advantages and Disadvantages of Co-dependency

Chapter 4: Psychological Impact of Co-dependency

Chapter 5: Seeking Help

Chapter 6: How to Help yourself along with your Loved One in Co-dependency

Chapter 7: Looking at Life Differently by focusing on yourself

Chapter 8: Finding Support Groups to help you on your recovery

Chapter 9: Resolving Issues of Self Help: Breaking Free of Depression and Inferiority Complexes

Chapter 10: Preventing future Co-dependencies and steps to stabilize your life

Chapter 11: Ending Co-dependency in a healthy way

Chapter 12: Dysfunctional relationships and Co-dependency

Chapter 13: Radical Reboot: Discovering Peace, Happiness and Contentment

Chapter 14: Conclusion

Highly Recommended Codependent Books

BONUS

Copyright 2014 by Globalized Healing, LLC - All rights reserved.

Chapter 1

Defining Co-dependency in Relationships

What is Co-dependency?

Co-dependency can be defined as an abnormally excessive psychological or emotional attachment to a partner (in any relationship), usually one with an addiction or disability; be it emotional, mental or physical. Co-dependency often appears to be a highly traditional relationship standard, one of caring for your partner and putting their needs before your own. Many co-dependents exude the virtues of nursing, support, love and affection and maintain these traits to be the very reasons to remain with an addict and as such continue to nurse their addictions in an effort to find that *thing* that makes them feel complete.

One note that should be made now; is to understand where co-dependency traits originate. Most frequently these traits are learned due to a long history of addiction, poor self-image, abuse and the lack of emotional fulfillment in ones formative years.

Some Characteristics and Examples of Co-dependency

Firstly, co-dependency consists of numerous traits, attitudes and behavioral characteristics which make it easy to identify in relation to other relationships. Co-dependency often starts out in a relationship when one partner develops and addiction to the traits of their partner, be it their partners own addiction or abusive behaviors and traits. When this happens, one partner becomes the enabler of the other, usually this happens gradually. In some relationships the addicted party finds their way gradually into recovery while the enabler is left to cope with the emotional and mental scars, patterns, and discontent or resentment of their relationship. Some of the most distinct examples of co-dependency are when on person is abnormally addicted to the negative behaviors or addictions of their partner to:

1) **Alcohol:**
   Living with an Alcoholic:

Sarah* is 25, she is successfully employed as the managing editor of a large magazine revolving around the entertainment industry, and in her off time she picks up work as a freelance writer for other industry publications. Her romantic life is deeply founded in her belief that even when in a relationship women should always remain independent. Sarah spent many years working with a therapist before making these decisions in regards to how she wanted her life and relationships to work. While Sarah would appear to be a success story, this is only because of her past and her ability to overcome co-dependency.

Just two short years ago Sarah was an intern working at a highly regarded local weekly paper. She was on the road to success; this publication had a reputation for only employing the most talented young journalists from all parts of the country. It was an honor for Sarah to get this position, and it was the first step in her dream to escape the small down monotony that she had known all her life. She had high aspirations for herself and saw herself as the shining star of journalism that every famous publication wished to hire. Shortly after starting her internship, she met Alex. He was older, more mature than the boys she had wasted her time dating, charming, and attractive. Sarah was smitten. Of course so was every other young female working in the office, drawn to his wit and wisdom no one seemed to notice the slight hint of whiskey on his breath. It was destined that Sarah would start dating Alex after they spent time working closely on a new formatting project and no one was surprised when they moved into his apartment a few weeks later, many of the old foundation staff had seen this happen before. Sarah was head over heals in love with Alex, spending all of her time taking care of him, showering with love and catering to his every whim. She made sure that he had all the luxuries he was used, and was determined to ensure that she was always there for him when he needed her. It didn't take long before his addiction crept out and took over their relationship, it was a rocky road and Sarah was far from prepared for the wild ride she was about to embark upon. Sarah was positive that if she provided him with regular company he would chose her over his love of whiskey. Slowly she became drawn to the care he needed when he was drinking, she liked the dizzy speed of life when they were out on the town. It all seemed manageable at first.

Then, one day, after returning home from the office, Sarah came home to find the house unlocked and Alex was no where to be found. It was in this moment that things suddenly became very real and inescapable. Alex's drinking had nearly turned deadly, the diagnosis was grim and Alex was faced with the decision to stop drinking altogether or he would surely die. It was a medical nightmare, for three months Alex found himself fighting his inner demons while in treatment. Sarah spent her days trying to hide her own drinking and her nights pacing the floor alone with her own liquid demon feeling lost and empty without Alex there to keep her spirits up soon she was drinking more than she ever had when Alex was home! In time Alex home, he has a new lease on life, and was ready to take on the world while Sarah was now trapped in the grasp of the buzz she had come to be so familiar with since he moved in with Alex. Reality was Alex had successfully stopped his relationship with alcohol...Sarah did not. After several weeks of pleading with Sarah to get the help that she needed and being told to mind his own business Alex broke things off and asked Sarah to move out. Sarah felt as if she had lost everything, her best friend, the man she loved, her home, and the very world itself. So, she drank until her own health seemed to be at risk. Eventually, someone cared enough for Sarah to insist that she get the help she needed to enter rehab herself and to remove her addictions from her life. It was a hard road but in the end, Sarah was free!

Alcohol addiction in co-dependency is cited as one of the most prevalent cause and effect indicators of problems in ones relationship. Statistics show that the wives of alcoholic men account for the highest percentage of co-dependent individuals in society. Why? At its core a co-dependent relationship is defined by one partner being addicted to the negative behavior of another to the detriment of the entire relationship.

We all have the right to liver our lives as we wish, partaking in the things that makes us happy or feel good, but we must always keep in mind that there is always a cost involved for the abuse/overuse of anything. The reality of this cost is often forgotten by the co-dependents as they grow in their addition to excess as well as to the need to be with one another for fear they would no survive alone!

2) Drugs:
Living with a chemically addicted partner

She was seventeen, and the memories that were soon to be made in college looked as if they would be the best moments of Elianna's* life. She had always dreamed of finding her college sweetheart and being swept up in the social scene of a big University. Life was not going to let her down, and once they met love was quick and overwhelming for Elianna and her crush Victor. They met during the second week of school at a fraternity party, in no time at all they were engaged and living together soon after. But there was a dark side to college life and in no time Elianna found herself struggling to keep her head above water, it was at this point in Elainna's life that she was introduce to the boost you could get from taking ADD meds when you didn't have the affliction. By the end of her freshman year she knew all the tricks to buy these prescription pills from other students. Everyone seemed to be doing it, friends and strangers got high all hours of the hours of the day. During her second year Elainna found the high she could get from pot and ecstasy were more than she could get from prescription meds. Life was constantly getting harder to cope with every day. As with any other addiction the use of a stimulant drug to cope will soon not only impact your own life, but the lives of those around you.

This impact would soon find its way into Elianna's life and that of her friends and family. College didn't get any easier with the help of even the strongest of drugs and Elianna was forced to leave college her grades had slipped and she no longer had the money to pay for her classes without the assistance of student loans that required good grades. Shortly after this Victor left her. She attempted to get a job and support herself, but her continued addiction led her to spend more than she earned each week. She knew that the drugs she was ingesting were harmful, but she didn't care, they were her escape from the painful reality of her life. No matter how momentary the escape was. When things started to look the grimmest and the high was no longer enough to hide the darkness around her Elianna sought to end it all with a needle in her arm. Elianna thankfully did not die, thanks to her best friend whom she had decided to call and say bye. Because of this friend Elianna found her way into rehab where she stayed for two years. Elianna has found the calm that she needed to escape from all the hardships of her past. She owns her own home, and has found the strength to start her own business raising organic crops from her small farm. Rehab, opened her eyes to many things. She knows that as always she has the right to decide what she will do with the moments of her life.

3) Sex:
Living with a Sex Addict

Alaine and Dan had dated for four years, it was the longest relationship she has ever had, and when he broke up with her she was devastated. She had never imagined that life would be anything but the perfect picture she had painted for herself. Growing old with Dan was all she hoped for. When he was gone Alaine found she missed the emotional and physical bonds that they had once with Dan. She envied her friends carefree dating life, spending time with men she had just met. Some she would see again, but most were merely one night stands. They often talked about the topic of dating and how sex was not necessarily something to be denied simply because you had not met your sole mate. Then one night at a party, she decided it was time to throw caution to the wind and she hooked up for the night with a cute guy she'd never seen before. They found themselves at a sleazy hotel where they spent hours having the best sex that Aliane had ever had. The thrill had hit its mark.

Aliane was overjoyed, she couldn't thank her friend enough for her words of encouragement and shared ever aspect of the wild trip she had started upon.

A month went past and another, then one day Alaine woke up body aching feeling used and not having recalled having been with a man in a room that she didn't recognize. Many men had found their way into their bed, and many had tried to have a relationship with Alaine. Each one was met with the same response…"It's been fun, but it's just not going to work. I have needs that you just can't fulfill"

Aliane was caught up in the thrill; it didn't matter where she got it man or woman. Some times multiple partners in one night were still not enough to fill her needs. No more was it just the thrill of the sex, it was the thrill of getting caught, or the carefree thrill of having unprotected sex because it felt better for her and her partner. She threw caution to the wind and refused to use contraceptives of any kind. It was no longer a rush to have sex with as many people as possible it was a physical need that must be met. Until the day she woke up exhausted, unable to move, coughing racked her body and blood ran from her nose. It took all she had just to crawl to the phone and call an ambulance. The paramedics found her passed out on the floor. After three days in ICU the diagnosis was grim, Aliane had contracted AIDS and was now suffering from pneumonia. Forced into a life of celibacy depression soon took over her life and she was faced with months of therapy to feel whole again.

This is not to say that sex is bad, it is far from it. The mutual enjoyment that comes from intercourse is one that should be shared with someone you love. A healthy sexual appetite in a relationship is a good thing, it is an emotional bond unlike any other, but being smart and practicing safe sexual practices should always be a priority. For your own mental health, never be a slave to your physical desires!

4) Parent-Child relationships:
Co-dependency in Children

One of the most natural and potentially most harmful of co-dependencies exists in the relationship between a parent and child or child and a sibling. The addiction in this case does not owe itself to a substance, but instead to a sense of security of ones family. Dependency of a child upon a parent for the fulfillment of emotional stability during our youth may seem to be sweet or endearing to a parent. However, in the view of a child, this is a fear that arises from the worry of being abandoned by their parent or being unable to satisfy the dreams the parent has for them. This can lead to issues of homesickness, panic-attacks and depression for a child causing him to fear they may be alone forever. The child may find that they are incapable of making their own decisions regarding the simplest of things, or frozen with fear when out of the parent's presence during their formative years.

Co-dependency in Parents:

Another form of co-dependency in the Parent-child relationship is one in which the parent forms a dependency upon their child, and the child the enabler. In case of many parents, the mistakes lie in acts of over-protectiveness. This is not to say that a parent should not be protective over there children. However when afraid to permit their child to take an escorted flight to visit their grandparents in a distant city because of the chance that the flight may crash this is a sign that the parent may be exhibiting over-protective tendencies as they are overly concerned over something that is in all probability unlikely to occur. This behavior and anxiety should be with counseling and therapeutic care. Sometimes parents stress too much over their children's career plans as a resultant idea of their own life experiences, hence, the child loses his own identity in their desire to please their parent. Many a times, parents are the ones who neglect a kid's innate desire to choose a career out of his own interest, which leaves the child filled with resentment and the urge to rebel against the career in which they find themselves.

Children do not come with handbooks, and parents are not given users manuals to aid them in the proper care and raising of a child. If you become a parent remember that your child is a separate entity from yourself and should be allowed to grow as a unique individual separate from you. Teach them to live their lives not yours, and show them the tools they will need to be successful in life.

5) Mental or Physical Disabilities:
Mental Disabilities:
Living with an OCD-Person

Dave had just taken a position in a new office when he happened to meet the girl of his dreams, Elissa. Dave and Elissa met and found they shared a crazy view of life at an office Annual Party. Dave had recently suffered a break up and was in a rush to begin dating once, and Elissa happened to be just the spark that drew him in. Elissa moved in with Dave little by little and at every step of the way, Elissa showed signs of discomfort until Dave allowed her to rearrange the apartment to her standards. Within a few short weeks, Dave's apartment had a new order to it. "A place for everything, and everything in its place." Dave learned the things that triggered Elissa's anxiety and he himself began to become overly critical regarding cleaning the already pristine floors, straightening the wrinkles on the bed and organizing the freezer just so. Elissa and Dave had a huge fight and she moved out. There were no attempts at reconciliation, however, Dave was convinced if he was able to achieve the results she desired she would come back on her own accord. The biggest change in Dave came when he became so brutally obsessed with cleaning and organizing the apartment that is consumed his entire life even keeping him from going to work. His obsession became so intense that getting Elissa back was his only thought…but that speck of dust in the air kept him from her.

His colleagues visited him and talked to Dave, he promised them he would come to work, but nothing of the sort happened. Dave continued to find a sense of calm only when he was able to clean. One day, his friend Maria visited him and managed to drag him to a psychiatrist. The doctor was confident that in time they could work out a plan to resolve Dave's disorder. The therapy worked and Dave showed a significant change in the span of less than a month.

OCD in regards to cleanliness is one of the many virtues that make a person become alert or enlightened about the order, hygiene and healthy aspects of things, irrespective of their size. The obsession can be about anything and co-dependency clearly states that obsession because of anything on an abnormal basis leads to a bad behavior of craving or needing that affects mentally.

Living with a Schizophrenic

Another potential trait of a person in co-dependent relationships is the aspect of feeling that they are the sole support of the disabled. One in which the responsibilities of caring for a partner is what drives the other partner to excessively provide for the needs of the other. The feeling is more than love as it is started mainly based on a sympathetic bond. The enabler provides compassion and love in unbiased proportions so much so that the survival of both becomes impossible without the other. Love is merely a façade in this case.

Schizophrenia for example should be treated as quickly as it is discovered. A schizophrenic needs professional help not just heavy dosages of compassion and coddling. As time goes on and the disorder is not treated the enabler finds themselves to be resentful of the dependent in their life and depression is sure to seep into their life. Eventually, there comes a point when the schizophrenic seeks out medical help. The enabler however, does not. This is a very dangerous position to be in.

Living with a Bi-polar or Suicidal Partner

Perhaps one of the hardest aspects of any relationship to over come is when one partner is overcome by such a strong mental or emotional state that they are unable to explain or even comprehend what it is that is going on in their own life. In the case of a Bi-Polar or Suicidal partner the emotional state of the partner is unpredictable and when left untreated…deadly. This forces the enabler to become an interpreter for their partner. Trying to understand their partner's needs and emotions while also maintaining a sense of sanity for them both is debilitating.

In case of Physical Disabilities:

Living with the paralyzed victim of an accident is one of the many situations that is most often portrayed in films and televisions. Impairment during an accident renders the partner to instantly take on the role of enabler mode. It is a fine line between healthy and co-dependency. The physicality of the events is usually genuine from both sides. However, the trauma can induce certain behavioral changes in the victim as well as the partner. Certain outbursts of anger, verbal or physical abuse, withdrawal and isolation all occur and create distress in even the strongest relationship. .

There are many examples of how an enabler's life can be stressed even long after the dependent is out of the picture. The focus of their lives while on some level is natural and ordinary other aspects are the result of past relations in which they participated in co-dependent behaviors rather than those of genuine love. Some of the practical examples of co-dependency can be seen in human characteristics such as seeking behavior, looking for love, friendship, companionship, the desire to care for someone in need, drowning their emotions in food, and eventually humility. In addition, a co-dependent chooses to vent out this specific frustration and undue pressure using many other ways. Some of them can be heavy, but everything can be managed if help is sought sooner.

Chapter 2

Recognizing Co-dependency: Quizzes, Symptoms and Characteristics for the Co-dependent

As we grow each generation believes in the right to determine what they will or will not do, it is their god given right to chose the road they will go down, as such decisions are made and experiences lived it is not immediately evident who will or will not become a co-dependent. Masochism is one possible sign of a co-dependency that is the desire to feel pain at the hands of another in order to gains sexual or emotional satisfaction, then perhaps we have an explanation for why some individuals chose BDSM (Bondage Discipline Sadism and Masochism) as a way of life. Depression and bi-polar disorder have increased annually, in some cases as a result of our fear of abandonment, failure and our incapability of coping with the same. Each of us copes in a different way to our emotions. Often, during the most trying of times, we forget about or ignore the bigger picture of not just surviving but of 'living'.

First step of Recognition of Co-dependency: Quiz

Answer in true or false answers only.

1. My current significant partner is addicted to a substance.
2. My current significant partner is addicted to sex.
3. My current significant partner is addicted to food.
4. My current significant partner is physically or mentally disabled.
5. I cannot take personal criticism.
6. I feel like a savior whose shoulders are burdened with the weight of the world.
7. I either trust too much or none at all.

8. I'm frightened of being in a crowd because I feel that I compare myself with others too much.
9. I'm frightened to introduce new girls to my partner.
10. I blindly buy my current significant partner's excuses, however impossible they are.
11. I feel exhausted and overwhelmed all of the time.
12. I do not know if I understand love or if what I believe is love is actually pity.
13. I'm a very defensive person.
14. My world revolves around the anxieties of my significant other.
15. I do not spend even half of my money on myself.
16. I'm starting to feel that I have developed an addiction of my own.
17. I feel at times that life has no purpose.
18. I fail at almost all resolutions I take.
19. I often feel that I don't deserve to live.
20. Sometimes, I feel that if I die, my significant other will be happy.
21. I feel guilty when I see my significant other's distress.

If you can relate to the above or answered true to even a couple of the statements, then you have the potential to find yourself in a co-dependent relationship. If you answered more than five of the above answers as true then you have the potential not only of realizing that you are in a co-dependent relationship but you also are armed with the tools here to repair your relationship.

A co-dependent person allows their world to revolve around that of another. It is impossible to sustain this relationship sans the other person and if attempted, the world will appear to make no sense or will become meaningless. If co-dependency traits are recognized early in life, many relationships can be repaired and allowed to function in a healthy manner.

Symptoms of co-dependency

While the primary dysfunction in a co-dependent relationship is the overt attachment to the behavior of another there are many other symptoms that can assist in the detection of co-dependency in any relationship. Some of the symptoms of co-dependency are

   a. Abnormally Caring for others
   b. Low Self esteem
   c. Guilt
   d. Feelings of shame or embarrassment
   e. Attraction to charity and neediness
   f. Boredom/ Extreme stressed or disinterest in life
   g. Feel victimized
   h. Indecisiveness
   i. Belief in others more than the self
   j. Worthlessness
   k. Dysfunctional family relations
   l. Fear of rejection
   m. Fear of failure
   n. Pessimism
   o. Repression
   p. Obsessive behavior
   q. Going crazy in the absence of the other
   r. Insomnia
   s. Anxiety disorder
   t. Micro-management
   u. Depression

v. Equating love with pain
w. Begging
x. Coercion
y. Advise
z. Bribing

One of the biggest reasons for a co-dependent's improper alignment of emotions, thoughts and feelings are their poor communication skills. They have become so self-absorbed with the addictive behavior in their life that they often will say anything in order to get the results that they desire. Even when this means being deceptive, hiding the truth, or flat out lying in order to get their way. Manipulative communication and behavior patterns are how they survive. They have no concern for how their actions will impact others, they merely act as they wish and throw caution to the wind. Some of the feelings of obsession and abnormal desire to control arise from the desire to always make things better mixed in with a feeling of low self-esteem. Co-dependents often have very limited or flimsy boundaries for themselves and others. At certain times, the partner is blindly followed or even taken for granted as the co-dependent's mind is clouded with their own imaginary interrogations, answers and inferences. Co-dependents are indecisive, but, it does not mean that their decision-making slots are empty. The reason that a decision is impossible to make, is owed to the fact that too many thoughts swirl together and clog the same space. They use pain to focus and hence masochism or sadism are two significant virtues that can often be used when attempting to identify a co-dependent. The immediate reactions or responses of a co-dependent owes to their own insecurity. This is a result of their inability to trust their own thoughts or feelings. Another important sign of a co-dependent is the recurrent abuse of God or believing that God has abandoned their existence. Note that this is not a route to atheism, but a deeper sense of self-destruction where the co-dependent is absorbed by a feeling of worthlessness, uselessness or purposelessness!

Delving deeper, some of the emotions that repeatedly flash on a co-dependent are fear, anger, hurt, repression, control, obsession as all other emotions are misplaced or stunted. If the dysfunction in any relationship which leads to co-dependence is noticed, the former starts to portray a wider range of traits such as

- a. Exhaustion
- b. Fatigue
- c. Isolation
- d. Withdrawal
- e. Being alone
- f. Emotional/ Physical/ Mental Illness
- g. Psychosomatic illness
- h. Addiction to substances
- i. Hopelessness
- j. Suicidal thoughts or actions

Traits of the Co-dependent

a. In case of sexual, drug, alcohol or any addiction, a co-dependent feels that their own sense of control is escaping them, which will result in their embarrassment. A co-dependent is alert and conscious of what is going on around them, as well as worried about the possessive traits of their partner, draining their own emotional energy. A co-dependent adapts to a whining tone that reflects very little optimism or positivity. Life becomes granted too fast for a co-dependent that their sensitivity and display of emotions becomes too intense and random. They take care of the other regardless of their own desires. They lose all concepts of time and space, refuse any pleasure other than physical or emotional masochism, feel sexually revolted, feel pleasure but only in the technical sense and propagate a flimsy nature of abstinence towards pleasure outwardly. The blame game of the co-dependent affects their vocabulary and they start to speak in accusatory words such as, 'you made me feel...' or 'he makes me feel ....'

Some of the traits of co-dependent personalities are:

b. Incapability of comprehending Normalcy
c. Decrease in pleasure/ Finding no pleasure
d. Judgmental in regards to themselves as well as others
e. Low self-esteem and confidence
f. Emphatically blaming self or others for their mistakes
g. Chronic Lying
h. Abnormally sensitive to all criticism, especially personal
i. Tend to look out for distressed people, to be the caretaker in all things!
j. Rigidity in action, thoughts and behavior
k. Chaos-loving/ melodramatic
l. Fear of abandonment, hence people-pleasing
m. Denial of Sadness and Sorrow
n. Confused in differentiating pity and love.

Chapter 3

Advantages and Disadvantages of Co-dependency

When we look closely at the co-dependent we are often quick to judge and only see that dysfunction in their relationship. However, it is quickly forgotten that while this dysfunction is visible to us at its worst was most often rooted in the very foundation of one's love for their spouse, parent, or child. The question then becomes, when does one's love for their partner, parent or child turn from something wonderful to be cherished and becomes something dysfunctional?

Love for another and feelings of charity towards them are not often viewed as a disorder. However, the truth is that when the attachment towards another surpasses the norm to the point that we deny our own needs in order to provide for the selfish needs of our loved one, our feelings of self-worth and self-esteem are greatly diminished as a result. At times like these, it is right to conclude that there is something missing in our lives, am emptiness that we are looking to fill either one that we have had since childhood or one that has developed as a result of our past relationships. Either way once an individual has taken a turn down this path the emotional toll is vast.

Advantages of Co-dependency are certain uneven traits displayed towards the partner, like

1) Love
2) Responsibility
3) Caring
4) Peace
5) Assurance
6) Faith

7) Safety
8) Security
9) Support
10) Finance
11) Stability
12) Happiness
13) False Contentment

The advantages of co-dependent relationships are often momentary, the results of certain events which give rise to a favorable set of circumstances. These advantages can be achieved even in a co-dependent relationship if there is at some point a healthy attachment to each other, one in which the needs of both partners in a relationship participate. However, this does not stand to say that love alone is a valid reason to become obsessively possessive of one another. Certain experiences together such as intimacy are capable of creating the illusion of everything in our lives becoming magical, miraculous or eternal. But in reality, the danger in not being able to recognize when the attachment has crossed from normalcy, to dysfunction!

If you find a virus in your computer and it fails to function properly you do not continue to operate that machine hoping that it will fix itself, instead you backup your computer and take it in for repair before more damage a can be done. Just like repairing your computer, it is possible to seek out help and repair the "virus" that is a co-dependent relationship in order to attain a healthy relationship. There are so many forms of help available to those who wish to find it, therapists, support groups, 12 step programs, counselors, treatment centers and self help books. There is a tool to fit everyone's life and personal needs. All you need to do is take the first step and admit that you need help.

Disadvantages of Co-dependency

Now to come to the obvious side of the issue, co-dependency is evidently a high dosage of negativity that can mentally damage or impair not only you but all of those around you. If you're the co-dependent or not, it is undeniable at least one addiction or negative emotional force has become the centre of your world. This is not only an unhealthy relationship, but has the potential to cause further disruption to your emotional state with feelings of depression, distress or hopelessness.

The first disadvantage of co-dependency is that if you are incapable of tolerating any disapproval, then you're setting yourself up to be exposed to manipulation. We are all individuals, no matter who else is in our life, parents, children, spouses, significant others, our failures and our successes are purely ours and not the result of what we can do for others. Each of us has a different perspective on life and a different perception of life than every other person alive. Once we are gone, no one else will ever have this same perception again, because it was purely ours alone. If people are unable to be content as an individual, their life is going to be one rough ride. It also means that at the advent of any a relationship, good or bad, the intensity and the toxicity of the bond shared has a chance of being misunderstood by the co-dependent. It is to everyone's benefit to be aware of the signs that you are slipping into these negative trends and prevent them from harming you and your relationships.

Some of the most toxic disadvantages of co-dependency are:

1) Anger
2) Ownership
3) Commanding
4) Intolerance

5) Blame-game
6) Worthlessness
7) Strong Nihilism
8) Loneliness/ Abandonment
9) Undue pressure of responsibilities
10) Fear of everything
11) Recurrent panic attacks
12) Laziness
13) Exhaustion
14) Lethargy
15) Poverty
16) Contempt
17) Hatred towards people
18) Social-awkwardness
19) Possessiveness
20) Confusion
21) Paranoia
22) Low-self-esteem
23) Pessimism
24) Instability
25) Indecisiveness
26) Guilt
27) Rigidity
28) Chronic lying
29) Poor communication skills
30) Poor personal space/ boundaries
31) Abnormal dependency
32) Obsession
33) Repression

34) Lack of faith
35) Intimacy issues
36) Control-freak
37) Perfectionism
38) Drug/Sex/ Substance abuse
39) Critically sensitive to personal criticism
40) Suicidal tendencies

Chapter 4

Psychological Impact of Co-dependency

Now that you know what co-dependency is in realistic terms, you are armed with the tools to analyze how co-dependency originated in your life and relationships. Lennard J. Davis, the author of *Obsession: A History* pointed out the term co-dependency found it's way into our lives as a way to describe some who used their relationships with others as their main source of personal identity and internal value. He also noted that the historical patterns seen through those involved in Alcoholics Anonymous 12 step recovery program noted their addiction being compounded by a loved one who filled an enabling role in their life. This was on account of the fact that the enabler was in turn addicted to the feeling they got from caring for or sheltering the addict in their lives. A twisted dependency upon someone else's dependency upon them

Psychologists describe co-dependency as a condition where a person is desperately seeking their partner's approval in order to justify their own existence. Psychologists emphasizes that the attachment formed in a co-dependent relationship is much more complicated than the normal drive to be a care taker who makes personal sacrifices for their loved ones. The unhealthy extent of any attachment that takes you away from your own needs and values is an addiction in and of itself, and should be treated by a competent therapist or life couch in order to repair the individual. There are many cases today, of self-sacrifice that results from a genuine healthy place! Like a parent loving a child or a person loving their pet or a partner loving their closest loved one. These cases prove that in genuine times of need, when maintained in a healthy manner the case is not a co-dependency. It is when this start to take an unhealthy toll on anyone, the danger of permanent paralysis of self-esteem and hope happens and the doorway to co-dependency is thrown open.

Psychologists state that one party to a co-dependent relationship will normally take up the behavior of a maternal figure in their lives, picking up on the desire to be a care giver and to nurture those in their lives until they no longer recognize themselves and only the behaviors that they whish to exude. On the flip however it is not uncommon for co-dependents to also perceive of themselves as the victim of their partners needs and resentful of the demands upon them as well. In many circles, the co-dependent is often described incorrectly as a love addict who will go to any means to make their relationship appear to others to be perfect. They go to great lengths to ensure that they provide the needed material items to always look like a success even at the detriment of their own needs. These are signs that the co-dependent has accepted that these delusions of success are enough to prove their worth. These enablers often appear to be the martyrs of their relationship, exaggerating how much they have given into the relationship and how little it matters to the other. But it really is just a façade, the final failure of the relationship will come and when it does it is often accompanied by guilt, grief and resentment that they have spent so much of their time focusing on their partner in an effort to avoid abandonment, and often regretting the choices made so much as to wish they were no longer alive.

The psychological impacts of co-dependence include the following behaviors';

   a. Begging or pleading desperately with their partner to ensure they are never alone.
   b. Threatening or blackmailing their loved ones emotionally.
   c. Panic attacks at the thought of being alone.

d. Chronic lying
e. Making a melodramatic attempt to guilt their partner into staying with them
f. Faking pregnancy to keep a partner
g. Creating a financial dependence upon themselves in and effort to control their partner.
h. Dangerous sexual experimentation
i. Unending resolutions to impart change
j. Suicidal tendencies as a result of extreme hopelessness, depression and loneliness

Psychological impact of Unaddressed Co-dependency

Psychologists believe the first signs of co-dependency lie in the human nature that provides for the belief that their ones ideologies and doctrines are intone with to another or the belief that they can shape another into a image similar to that of themselves. In other cases of co-dependency there is the trap of victimization, this belief is rooted in our psyche placed there through our past when we felt complete because of someone else's validation of us. Who would deny that it feels good to have someone say, 'you make me feel so special', 'no one has made me feel loved the way you do', or 'you have made us so proud!' Our subconscious thrives on the understanding that it is possible for us to create change and make a positive impact on those around us. It is human nature to want to be around other people, it's better to be with someone who doesn't value us than it is to be alone. Hence, the fear of abandonment pulls on us into relationships rather than allowing us to take the time to seek out the one who is right for us, and will treat us the way we deserve. Co-dependency is defined by the dysfunction caused by having many inner conflicts simultaneously. When our subconscious focuses upon these moments in life as the only ones in which the stars aligned and we felt complete, then we take on the traits that we portrayed in those moments. As the co-dependent goes through life this becomes all they know, their inner self is unable to find any other way out of this cage they have built for themselves. This inner self eventually withers or wilts off with recurrent dissatisfaction, discontent and depression.

Some of the unaddressed co-dependencies include:

1. **Negative extremities:** in the course of treating a co-dependent to recognize the source of their low self-esteem and repressions, the treatment may cause moments of aggressive behavior, impatience or denial. This usually happens when there is no proper manner of recovery and the person is forced to blindly change and become the opposite of what they have always been.

    Example:

    > Rick is 9 years old, a small little boy in the 4th grade who is picked on often. His best friend is a 5th grade boy named Mickey, who just happens to be the largest boy in their school. While they seem to have nothing in common Mickey and Rick formed their friendship many years ago as they have been neighbors all their lives. Mickey is the class bully, who bullies everyone in the class except Rick. This is not to say that Rick is protected from others who would bully him. Mickey has aspirations of hanging out with the big kids from the middle school, and when he hands out with these big kids he often brings Rick along and offers him up as a scapegoat, something of a sacrifice to older gods of the middle school. Rick has never told anyone what Mickey has done to him, but

his whole class knows. Time goes by and Rick becomes more and more intent on changing his place in life, he will no longer be the one that all the bullies pick on in school. Soon, Rick is the oldest boy in the middle school, no one picks on him any more...however, sadly Rick himself is now the bully that he himself dreaded being around.

Rick is no longer the victim in the co-dependent relationship, he's been pushed around long enough and determined he would no longer be in this position. Unfortunately he had no leadership, no one to help him down the road to recovery; as a result he has become the thing he most detested.

2. **Victimized:** Individuals who find themselves in a co-dependent relationship will often feel that they are always the victim, it's not their fault they are in this relationship, it is their partners fault. They can't leave, or their partner will surely not be able to survive. They have no choice but to be trapped. This is not an attractive place to be, and on that will most often bring about embarrassment and shame so they hide the truth from those around them. This leads them to develop a habit of keeping all of their feelings of stress and dissatisfaction sealed away inside them.

Example:

Seline has been dating Martin a senior in her college for almost three years now and can't imagine her life without him. Martin, however, is not nearly as attached to Seline sure she's fun to hang out with and the sex is great, she comes from a wealthy family and always has the newest technology and a fridge full of food. Over the last few months however Seline has started to feel that Martin's behavior has become erratic and that he is looking for someone to cater to his needs like a mother always picking up after him, cooking for him, and taking care of his laundry. Mutual friends have started to notice this trend and fear that things will go bad if the couple decides to live together. But Seline is not to be swayed, she really wants to make this relationship work and if that means being a mother to Martin until he matures then that is what she will do.

Martin however did not step up to the plate; he isolated himself in his room with his computer and online games. He soon began to demand that Seline bring him food, beverages, and any other item he might desire to have. When Seline wished to go out with her friends she wasn't able to Martin needed her to keep the house clean, he had laundry that needed cleaned, and he would starve if not for her cooking his meals. As a result Seline became lonely and began inviting friends over to hang out with her. Several brought with them beer, vodka, and other alcoholic beverages. Seline found she was able to escape the reality of the prison she lived in when she drank and soon she was drinking alone...every moment of the day.

Unable to continue to support herself in school any longer she returned home to her parents and left Martin and his demanding ways behind her. It was not an easy road; Seline's parents would not allow her to continue down this destructive road and had her admitted to rehab.

Seline battled with her alcoholism as a result of her relationship with Martin, his demands were too much for her, and while she had hoped that by being the caring nurturing partner that he would change there was no chance of that happening with someone like him. It is important to understand that being the martyr in a relationship is not healthy.

3. **Savior:** another potential result of an unaddressed co-dependency is that it is possible that a cruel or aggressive person can become so embarrassed by his own behavior that he became a savior instead. This excess within a co-dependency has proved damaging to one or both individuals and quite often continues to go unaddressed. In recovery when attempting to stabilize the dysfunction, one might see the error in their ways and start feeling as if they need to spend more time and effort caring for their family. Initially this may seem as if they are paying a penance for the awful way they have treated their family. But without the proper treatment and guidance this behavior is likely to become more habitual and the nurturing behavior may begin to increase to a point in which it cannot be controlled.

4. **Dysfunctional Families:** quite often the cause and effect of co-dependency can be traced back to childhood, when the hopes and expectation of the whole family are not met, naturally dysfunction arises. Poor communication skills are one of the many reasons for dysfunctional families.

    Sometimes, certain circumstances give rise to reasonless arguments, misunderstanding and hurt feelings because of a lack of clear communication among family members. Most families choose to ignore this behavior unaware how this important decision will impact the family. Long-term misunderstandings can end up creating a wedge of separation inside a once successful family unit. This develops a severe fear of abandonment and failure that may result in loosing contact with one another, even when residing in the same house!

5. **Improper Diagnosis:** another important aspect of diagnosing co-dependency holds with diagnosing it improperly. Many of the symptoms of co-dependency have a parallel within other psychological dysfunctions. Some situations can drive people to believe that their own relationship is nothing like a co-dependency it instead is a normal relationship in which only one party has a dysfunction! Others believe that there is such a thing as a healthy co-dependency, or shall we say a co-existence rather than a co-dependency. However, whenever an addiction is entertained for the survival of any other bond, co-dependency becomes a true and valid concern. Simply put, there is no healthy co-dependency.

Psychological recovery

Psychologists recommend two main methods of recovery for the co-dependent relationship. The first focus is on establishing a foundation for recovery that will be able to stand strong regardless of how long the recovery takes. These are:

a. Accepting the present, and putting the past where it belongs. Behind you! And begin your journey into the future. Think in terms of now and what is to come.
b. Recognize that you have the power to make your own decisions, rather than allowing another's thoughts and desires to be your only influence when making decisions; big and small.

Chapter 5

Seeking Help

How to seek Help

When there comes a time that you realize that your desires are not longer your own but are instead controlled by an external force that has crept into your relationship, or that someone in your life has created an abnormal attachment to you that has begun to influence your actions, this is when it's time to step back and reclaim your life. As we have seen the disadvantages of co-dependency will have only negative impacts upon your life, with the proper guidance you'll find that you are able to take control once more and become the person you have always wanted to be. It is to be expected that this will be a difficult journey, both for you and the co-dependent in your life, a journey will be rough at times but the reward will be great. While there area great number of self-help books available regarding this topic, we do suggest that you seek out professional assistance before taking on any form of recovery.

It is necessary to understand the adverse effects of co-dependency. Being armed with knowledge regarding what you are going through, as well as what to expect during recovery will speed up the process for you and your partner. If you go into this blindly you're sure to have a much more difficult recovery.

When our own internal desire to seek out happiness in the things that we do and allow only the negative to consume us, we fail to see that there is hope. Our decisions are no longer our own, they are founded in the actions of another. If the relationships dysfunction is not immediately handled, it is likely that what could be a momentary affliction will be life altering.

The reality is that if allowed to progress too far, it may very well be too late to repair. This does not mean that you should avoid recovery, because sometimes the hardest step to recovery is to realize you need to walk away because there is no way to salvage the relationship. Seek, help....now. Seek help with the help of others or on your own, whichever is more comfortable for you. But please find someone who is trained in the treatment of co-dependence and make the changes needed in order to find the happiness and self-worth that you deserve.

The following is a list of ways to seek help for your relationship, and yourself.

The first step to seeking help for a co-dependence, is to admit that you yourself are co-dependent

The most basic step to freeing yourself from the clutches of co-dependency is to look into your heart and embrace the fact that your current relationship is dysfunctional in its co-dependence and that you are ready to make a change. Only once that conviction has been realized can any potential for improvement begin. This moment marks the moment that you have declared that your life will be yours once more!

Once you clearly understand what is happening in your life and relationship, it can be difficult if not impossible to fully accept on the most basic levels. Denial is likely to creep in and add to the dysfunction of your relationship with your partner, the professional that you have sought assistance from and yourself. When you clearly realize what has become of your life and recognize the negative impact it has had on your daily existence you will slowly realize just how completely your life has been destroyed by this dysfunction and how imperative it is to move forward with recovery.

Take a moment and remember what your life was like before your relationship, when if first started, and where it is now. Write it down, the good, the bad, and the things you enjoy as well as the things you don't, no matter how trivial it may seem to you now or how badly it hurts to face in black and white.

Now, write down everything you wish to have in your relationship even if it means you will no longer be with the same partner. Write this as clearly as possible. Visualize it!

The second step to recovery is to properly understand the roots of your co-dependency.

The second step to freeing yourself from co-dependency is to look into your past and discover the very foundation of the dysfunction that has taken over your life.

Start by reviewing the notes you wrote previously regarding how your relationship has changed over time. Take a moment to note what these thoughts made you feel at the time, and how they make you feel now. Let out the emotions you've had bottled up for far too long, and get down to the bottom of your hurt, anger, self-loathing, and loneliness. What is it about these moments that caused these feelings, what could have changed the outcome?

Now, look at each of these memories and pick out your behaviors, which ones were reckless, which erratic, which well thought out, and how many caused harm of hurt feelings for a loved one? List the virtues that caused these damaging actions and circle them for good measure. These are the things we want to focus on removing from your life.

Review these frequently, and prepare yourself to confront them fact to face.

The third step is to evaluate why the relationship is bad for you as well as your loved one.

Now, consider both yourself and your partner and determine what aspects of your relationship are beneficial to you both, what harms you, what harms the other party, and what is harmful to your relationship as a whole. List the reasons for each of your worries. You should do this exercise with the least amount of bias as possible. Be honest with yourself, no matter how painful it may be. Write it down and think of arguments for or against all of your worries, which ones are going to be the hardest to over come, which the easiest, list them with the ones that cause you the least worry first and those with the most worry or anxiety last.

The fourth step is to talk to your partner.

With all these thoughts put together on paper, you've made steps in the right direction towards your own recovery; the next step is to determine if your ideas are ones that your partner is able to embrace as well. So, go to your partner and talk about all that you are thinking and what you hope to accomplish in order to repair you relationship and resolve its conflicts.

Start by talking-out your side of the relationship and all that you have recorded through your previous analysis as well as the rebuttal of reasons and resolutions. Listen to your partner thoroughly and heed their replies. Resist the urge to become argumentative, negative, or accusatory. Make note of their concerns, feelings, and accusations Do not make promises to instigate change, this is only a moment in time to share your thoughts and seek out your partners input on the current state of your relationship.

The fifth step is to reach an agreement regarding the changes your relationship needs to take.

Take the time to discuss everything you have on your mind, regardless of its intensity and rightness. Brainstorm together for resolutions that you can both agree upon as well as ones that you may not both agree to. Think each suggesting through without bias. Always being aware of the self-destructive habits that have surrounded your relationship for so long and the advantages of breaking free of them! If you find this step is unsuccessful then it's time to move on to the next step.

The sixth step is to seek help from a professional

The final step for you is to consult with a professional trained in co-dependence and addiction, do this together as a couple if possible, choose an individual who is familiar with these dysfunctions and who has no bias towards either of you. In the event that your partner is unwilling to seek treatment with you, then perhaps it is time for you to seek individual treatment to separate yourself from the relationship and partner who have caused you such great pain and suffering.

Chapter 6

How to help yourself along with your Loved One in Co-dependency

Think about a situation in which you are frustrated, exhausted and too drained to do any more for your relationship. Your financial stability as well as emotional composure is dwindling owing to your partner's unbendable addiction. If you were to attempt to cut off your partner's supply of their addiction of choice, the likely result would bring irritation and withdrawal for the both of you.

Helping yourself

1. <u>Reclaim yourself by believing in yourself</u>

Co-dependency is a toxic aspect of some relationships that is based on one's disbelief in themselves and their own self worth. This can also happen as a result of memories of abandonment along with the fear of experiencing the same in future relationships. The basic malfunction in a co-dependent relationship is the indecisiveness and fear of the co-dependent as a result of their need to cater to and nurture their partner's negative behaviors. In order to start repairing the relationship, both partners need to reclaim their own ideologies, interests, likes and dislikes, free from any influence e of the other. Only when we find our own road to happiness, shall we understand what it is to truly live. When you understand that the relationship is damaging to one or the both of you and you have already sought out solutions to no avail is when the time to move on needs to be considered. Once you start down the road to finding your true inner self, to fulfill your wishes, hopes, and dreams the rest of the journey will be easy.

Start your healing journey by listing out the biggest decisions you have made since you started your relationship. Jot down what your hopes and dreams for the relationship were as well as any concerns you've had along the way. Consider the moments in which you expressed your valid concerns clearly, as well as those in which it you were much too vague. Think over the times when you sacrificed your wishes for the other, and felt elated, exhilarated or joyous about it. The journey to find one's self starts from belief in one's self. Without realizing your own interests and irritations, it is impossible to understand one's self completely. Our feelings, emotions and reflexes are the map to our life and where it should go from the time we enter this world until we find our end. Take the time to reclaim yourself by examining your life and the direction you wish for it to go without the influence of others around you. Explore your own interests, don't be afraid to strike out and do the things that you enjoy the most and never be afraid of travelling and exploring the world around you. Take up a new hobby, find the things that drive you and pursue them.

Remember, life is but a bride waiting for you to make her smile. Don't look at life and blame her for your insecurities and troubles, take control of your own destiny and make this the life that you deserve and crave.

2. *Some exercises*

Some of the exercises that will help you become the person you were always meant to be include:

    a. Read as much as you can regarding co-dependency
    b. When you start feel panic slipping in, distract yourself. Go for a walk, read a book, sing a song, anything to take your mind off the anxiety that you are experiencing.

c. Write down your hobbies and pursue them!
d. Looking for the positives in your life.
e. Celebrate life by living it the way you want!
f. When you feel that a criticism is too harsh, stand up for yourself and your beliefs..
g. Speak out against people who try to control or take charge of you.
h. Believe that all feelings are just.
i. Don't be afraid to say no.
j. Be genuine as much as you can, even if it becomes a rant!
k. Open up to the people you find comfort in spending time with.
l. Finally, live and let live!

3. *Increase your self esteem*

One of the most important aspects of helping yourself not just to break away from co-dependency, but to also prevent it from returning to your life is to work on your self-esteem, confidence and assertiveness. It will be uncomfortable at first, after all assertiveness will happen only when a strong sense of self-respect has been reawakened from your subconscious. Often, we lack the conviction to confidently assert what is good for us, without allowing external forces to influence our decisions and actions. It's time to look at your life and realize that no one will ever love you as you deserve, if you cannot love yourself. This is a harsh adjustment from the manner in which most co-dependents function. Take your time, and do not rush yourself, it's your recovery and your well-being at stake, give it the time it deserves to allow for proper healing.

Some of the exercises to do to increase your self-esteem are:

- Stopping negative conversations with yourself: first and foremost, perhaps the hardest part of your journey is to stop telling yourself that you are not good enough, not worthy, or that this is an impossible change.

- Assertiveness: take a moment to realize that your opinions matter, voice them, and stand up for yourself.

- Realizing own dreams and ambitions: by exploring oneself through Meditation and relaxation exercises

4. De-addiction/Detoxification

It is crucial to your recovery that you leave all toxic aspects of your relationship behind you. Only when you are able to remove any chemical, emotional, or physical addictions from your life will you truly be freed from the dysfunction and harmful side of your relationship. As long as you or your partner remains addicted you will never be able to face recovery and repair the damage that has been done. This may very well be the first step for some co-dependents, addressing the addiction that has impacted your lives and removing it via treatment or rehab before being able to tackle your co-dependent relationship. Many people find that once recovery has been started on an emotional level that they are able to heal more quickly from the psychological aspects by also partaking in a full body detox, if you chose to go this route please consult with your health care professional prior to taking on any detoxification program.

5. Seeking the help of a trained professional

When things feel as if they have spun out of hand, and you don't know where to turn, do not be afraid to seek the help of a professional such as a psychiatrist, life coach or a recovered co-dependent. Even then if you find that none of your actions have improved the situation, consider leaving the relationship, as this may be the only way to completely recover from your co-dependence.

Helping your loved one

If you have any hope of making your relationship healthy once again, it is imperative that you not only ensure that you have your own needs taken care of but that you are providing healthy support to your loved ones. It is a fine line to walk to ensure that you are giving the love and support they need without shifting your enabling to another aspect of their lives. Know your boundaries, seek the assistance of a professional, and be prepared to walk away if there are no clear signs of progress in their recovery.

One of the most important things to be aware of is the topic of Self Care. Self-care is not only important to the recovery of an addict but also to their partner as well. The focus of self-care lies in recognizing the need to be independent and asserting your own opinions and dreams clearly and confidently.

Spend time with your partner, discuss what you've found regarding co-dependency and encourage them to spend time learning about co-dependence and sharing what they've learned with you. Be prepared to accept each other's differences in perspectives, ideologies and expectations it's ok to disagree just so long as you both are able to share and compromise to achieve recovery together. Only when you have both accepted the road to recovery is possible will you be able to work together to repair your relationship completely. Progress is possible when you both have the conviction to heal and improve yourselves rather than being an echo the other's decisions.

Some of the main ideas that you should be cultivating are:

a. **Autonomy:** demonstrate the right to govern your own life. Each of us has the God given right to direct our own life, no one else holds this power for or over us. When we understand that we are enslaved to no one for our emotional, mental or physical well being then we are ready to move forward with our life.

b. **Genuineness:** with oneself; no one can read our minds for us, just as we are unable to hide our true feelings from our deepest inner self. Stop lying to yourself regarding your relationship; you cannot hide the truth from the one person who sees into your soul…you! When a person knows who they are, and are genuine to themselves anything is possible.

c. **Intimacy:** the ability to open-up your heart and soul to another person is very difficult. It is nearly impossible to open up to a person who has caused you to struggle with your own inner self. Intimacy issues creep up from the past and it is very hard for many people in co-dependent relationships not to slip into old patterns. However, it is important if you wish to maintain your relationship that you not allow your intimacy to slip out of the relationship. It is our fears of abandonment, betrayal and failures that prevent this from being an easy step in our recovery. The most important part of intimacy is letting another person see you for the person that you really are, through your eyes so to speak. Open your heart up to your partner and allow them to see the raw side of yourself that no one else has the privilege of seeing.

d. **Abstinence:** from all addictions, from chemical abuse, to self-loathing behavior, and masochism; the addicted as well as the co-dependent must abstain from any of the harmful behaviors that brought them to this point in their lives and relationships. Only when abstinence to all addictions as well as controlling materials has been withdrawn from the relationship is recovery success possible. Sobriety is a necessity for the recovery of co-dependency. Healthy ways of satisfying your wants, dreams and hopes are possible only by being 'in control' and self-directed.

e. **Awareness:** about the condition of the relationship you and your loved one are in. This involves seeking awareness regarding your relationships dysfunction. In our discovery and the learning about our relationships, the awareness of our relationship may become so overwhelming that we need to seek help from a professional to resolve your conflicts in the most successful ways. There is NOTHING wrong with this.

f. **Acceptance:** of the fact that something needs to be done for the emotional and mental dysfunction to stop. Acceptance that your relationship is toxic and needs to change in order for you to find a healthy place for you and your partner.

Chapter 7

Looking at Life differently by focusing on yourself

In all aspects of recovery, you must always remember to focus on yourself. In a co-dependent relationship, both partners need to realize that focusing on your own well being is not selfish, or narcissistic but a vital trait to succeed in recovery. Co-existence makes two people transform their individual ideologies for the common good without departing from their own desires.

Focusing on yourself:

#1 Cultivating Assertiveness

The first step to leaving co-dependency behind you is to start cultivating assertiveness. Assertiveness is possible to articulate only when a person is sure about his own opinions and decisions. In order to start strengthening your resolve, one must learn to speak up, and be clear about what is on their mind. Don't be afraid to assert your ideas wherever or whenever you are. When one starts to articulate their thoughts, values, and concerns confidently and without judgment, then assertiveness becomes a virtue. In order to start having your own convictions, you should know ourselves, cultivate opinions of yourself and voice it aloud!

This is assertiveness.

When your partner has taken for granted that you have worked a 60 hour week, cleaned the house, cooked dinner every night, and demands that you put your book down get dressed up and ready for a night on the town, do not be afraid to say NO! But do so in a manner that does not put the blame on your partner. Tell you partner you are tired, you've had a long week and were looking forward to a night at home. And then, let them know that you are ok with them going out with thief friends. After all, you both need to have your own interests, friends and free time!

#2 Realizing one's Dreams and Ambitions

Each of us has our own dreams and ambitions. Only through a concentrated effort can a person realize one's own dreams, hopes and ambitions.

In a long term or dedicated relationship, there comes a time when every decision you make must consider the common good, however, at no time should you completely give up your dreams and ambitions. Change your time line to a more reasonable one, but continue to move towards your goals. This allows for a gradual movement to be made in the direction you wish to go, while not denying your partner the same experience in their own. Compromise, not giving in to them and shunning your own ambitions will lead to relationship success and recovery.

#3 Loving Oneself

In order to love yourself you must embrace the uniqueness that is YOU and no one else. Your life is made up of a million experiences, heart aches and celebrations, each one adds to the others in away that make you....you.

Always embrace who you are, and know that you are the one and only one who will ever be able to fully love you. Until you love yourself completely no one else will be able to do so, because you will hide your true self away from them. Some of the things to do to love yourself are, set goals, reward yourself, stop negative self-talks and go at things slowly!

#4 Transforming Perceptions

On your journey to recovery you will find you experience many changes to your ideologies and perceptions, this is healthy and to be expected. When an individual starts to focus on their own interests and wishes, their perceptions take a new light. Mostly, it widens and we start to understand so much more about ourselves and our priorities.

#5 Becoming emotionally Honest

Another important change that you should expect is emotional honesty. When we stop hiding our feelings, we overcome our mental constraints and return down the path to being happy again. Becoming emotionally honest entails authenticity clarity. This involves staying in touch with one's inner feelings, reactions to events and emotions. This results in a heightened sensitivity, external honesty and intimacy in all of our relationships. You must put aside the urge to continue in the self-manipulation and fear of losing control that are prevalent when you first begin to hide your emotions from those around you and then eventually yourself. In other words, if you are mad, say you are mad, embrace your anger and allow it to become a part of you, don't shove it off into a box and allow it to fester, you will do no one any good this way. But on the same token, do not be afraid to be happy and allow the world to know it.

#6 Explore your inner self

When you change your focus from the external stimulus around you and focus on your inner self you should respect all of the changes you experience in your own thoughts, feelings, and interests. This is normal personal growth and should be encouraged. Remember, that your goal is to be a complete and whole person in your own right without the influence of others around you.

#7 Spiritual Development

Part of exploring yourself is growing, finding new interests, learning new things, and opening you're heart and mind to things that you may not have thought about before. Allow yourself to become distracted from life by new interests, read books, listen to music, go to church, see movies the opportunities are endless. As you are growing as an individual it is often a rough road you travel, there are hard times to come and in order to get through those you will need to find a centre, or ground that allows you to reconnect with the world you are such an important part of. Take a yoga class, join a bible study, or find a local book club, anything that allows you to connect with the world on a higher level. Look into yourself and spend quiet time in reflection practice relaxation techniques and calm your mind. Spirituality will allow you to achieve a sense of stability and sanity and can provide you with the enlightenment you seek to make yourself whole again.

#8 Meditation and Relaxation Exercises

One of the most effective tools available to reconnect with your subconscious, is meditation and relaxation exercises. These tools will not only soothe and calm your mind, but also assist you in ways of inner communication. It starts with a calm quiet place, a relaxing set of exercises that allow you to disconnect from the world and become one with your subconscious. Your potential is infinite and with meditation, spirituality, and deep inner soul searching, you will be provided with the strength you need to continue down a very difficult road. These are tools you can take with you anywhere, use any time, and continue to develop no matter what life brings you

#9 Forgive

Forgive, unconditionally the wrongs that have been committed against you, do not hold grudges. Keeping these toxic feelings inside will slow down your recover, when you allow the anger and pain to be released and then forgive the act that has drawn you down you are allowing yourself to move on and release the hurt that you have carried for so long.

Start by talking to the person you wish to forgive. Be genuine in your communication with them and resolve to let go of the wrong done you. This is not to say that you are allowing the person you are forgiving to walk all over you, this is you making the decision to move past the hurt and pain that you have suffered, forgiving them, and saying. I will not allow you to continue to treat me this way, I have forgiven you, I have not forgotten but I am not going to hold this against you forever we need to move past this and heal...together.

#10 Recognizing your Responsibilities

While it is important to forgive others for the wrongs they have committed in your life, you must also own your own behaviors and reactions. Accept that you are not perfect and have done things in the past that have had the potential to hurt your loved ones. Take responsibility for your past actions, and recognize that in the future you will also have responsibilities not only to yourself, but to your family and friends as well. Once you start to accept your responsibilities you take ownership of your life and relationships on a new level. This allows you to become more independent while still developing a relationship with others in a strong and healthy manner.

#11 When in doubt...ask

It is human nature to feel that we know everything, even when we look at other people it is our nature to assume that we know what another person is thinking. But misunderstandings happen, and you cannot be afraid to ask your loved ones for clarification. If you do not know how your partner feels you can't help them, you can't bond with them, and there will always be something missing. So, take the time to ensure that you understand you partner and where they are coming from.

#12 Embrace Change!

Growing up and becoming a mature functioning member of society also entails that everyone undergoes a gradual metamorphosis of both: external image that one projects and the internal manner in which one approaches the world. Embrace change as a positive thing, look at how you view the world and your relationship and if you find that you are distressed, exhausted or jaded, it is time that you take the next step and look for a change that allows you to live in peace with yourself, and your partner.

#13 Make yourself your priority

As said before part of caring for yourself is understanding that you are your own first priority. Often people end up prioritizing others, and leaving themselves behind. When you ignore yourself and make others your priority, you open the door for personal neglect.

#14 Take care of the Physical as well as the emotional

When we make the decision to embrace such a drastic change in our lives withdrawal symptoms can be experienced not only by the addict but the enabler as well. Stress in any situation can lead to over eating, lack of exercise, and poor sleep patterns which will only stand to do you harm physically as well as emotionally. In order to be emotionally healthy you must also be physically healthy, do not turn to food or lethargy to cope with your current situation. Eat a healthy meal, take a walk, and remember that you are important! A healthy mind lives in a healthy body. If you're looking for peace, start with your body. Go to the gym, exercise when you feel irritated and maintain a healthy diet.

#15 Cultivate genuine friendship

Quite often the co-dependent will find that they have placed themselves in a state of isolation, the life they live is one in which they are trying to shelter their partner or so ashamed of where they are that they sever friendships and lock themselves away with their demons. Recovery is a big change, one that you do not need to make alone. Seek out old friends you have lost touch with and reconnect. Join groups who have similar interests and make new friends. BE honest with them, do not hide who you are and allow those relationships to flourish.

In order to be content and peaceful with oneself, you need to establish friendships with others who have like interests and experiences. It is through our friends that we seek comfort, find motivations, and learn acceptance. Cultivating genuine friendship is the biggest keys to emotional, mental and physical well-being of any person. Having a thousand and more virtual friends is not the answer the same as having a handful of close personal friends that are always there for you, and you for them!

#16 Speak out against criticism

When criticism is thrown your way without sense, or logic, speak up and make you voice heard. Do not shuffle back into the corner, or cower like a beaten dog. Stand up and say, this is not right! Only when we start voicing our opinions aloud, will we grow our conviction stronger!

17 Cultivate your own hobbies!

All of us have or have had hobbies, interests and passion that were all our own. Only through active cultivation of these interests and hobbies can we start to differentiate our own personal dreams from those around us. Cultivating a hobby is a step towards becoming your own individual.

#18 Increasing Self-confidence

Another important step towards focusing on yourself includes increasing your sense of self-confidence. Increasing your self-confidence involves doing mind exercise, developing your self-esteem and improving your own individual sanity. If you feel that you are not confident about your opinions, beliefs and ideologies, it is time to start thinking why. Do no let anyone else's opinion damage your opinion of yourself, be in control of yourself. Cultivate your own experiences, rather than echoing someone else's tale of orgasms!

#19 Pamper yourself!

All too often the co-dependent is so focused on the care of another that they forget that they must also care for themselves. More so they forget how important it is to pamper yourself. Do not put yourself on the back burner so deeply that you are unable to enjoy the fine things in life. Treat yourself to something that is not a necessity and enjoy the decadence of doing something just for you, with no motivation other than to simply enjoy it!

#20 Taking occasional Breaks!

It is all too common for individuals to become so absorbed in the rat race of life as well as the desire to be successful in our careers that we forget to breathe. It's important to take a break now and again in order to refresh our minds and remain focused on our life. The movement towards recovery is exhausting one; and if we do not take the time to recover and refresh our minds we'll never be able to clearly see the place that we wish to inhabit.

21 Love your job and you'll never work a day in your life again

This is the time to reevaluate your life, looking at every aspect of your life and relationship. How did we get to this point? Quite often we can find a root too our troubles in our home as well as in our career. Are you happy in the job that you have? Or, does it drag you down and cause more discontent in your life? This is your time to recreate yourself, if you find that your job is causing you to participate in negative behaviors then it is time to take a look at your job and pursue your dreams, don't just walk into work and quit. Keep your job, income is important, but begin to look in earnest for a job in the industry that you love. You will find a new peace when all things are in balance.

22 Get high on life!

An important thing to consider when leaving addictive substances behind you is that as a past addict you are surely destined to find something else to fill the place of the drugs or alcohol that you once were addicted to. Be aware of this and you will find that sobriety has its own heightened sense of awareness but in a much more balanced way. All of us know of the virtue of experiencing our emotions, when we allow ourselves to find emotional honesty, we find that we are able to "get high on life". Enjoy the sun on your face; revel in the way a light rain smells, laugh as you walk in the snow. Slow down and enjoy the little things.

#23 Being Positive!

One of the hardest things you will ever have to do during your recovery is to stay on track and never give up. No matter how hard it gets, you absolutely must stay positive. By maintaining a positive outlook you will exude a positive energy into the universe and draw good things to you. If you maintain a negative attitude towards your life and recover then nothing good will ever come to you, you will have set yourself up for failure. Being positive takes a lot of guts, it's not easy to keep a positive momentum going when you feel like the world is crashing in around you. Keep your head up, take a deep breathe, and keep telling yourself, "This is just a small bump in the road, together we can achieve anything

#24 Being Independent

Becoming the strong, independent person you were meant to be is a vital requirement to becoming focused on yourself. When your priorities have changed sufficiently it will help you become free to explore your independence. There is an overwhelming sense of pride and accomplishment once you have reached a state of independence. Knowing that you can and will survive and do it well without the help of anyone else will signal the moment in time when you have truly become free of your co-dependence.

All of us are born into this world to be individuals separate and apart from all others. Being independent requires a vast amount of courage, however the pay off is great, knowing that you can face anything and everything that life has to throw your way. So, be free to be yourself, know that you do not need anyone else to survive that you can do it alone, and you will be on the road to Independence and freedom.

#25 Self Care

Self-care as we discussed before is the ability to see to your own needs, to be able to heal your own emotional wounds and to ensure that you are the primary focus in your life. This is not to say that you live a life of selfish behaviors and distance from others. A narcissistic person can and will provide high-end self-care for themselves to the detriment of everyone around them. This is not the goal you wish for yourself, you are seeking a balance between caring for yourself and sharing your life with those that you love. But know that you are the only person responsible you're your own care and growth; do not depend on anyone else to do these things for you. Self-care is a necessary aspect of living, as through the acts of growing up, we realize that it is within our sense of duties to care for ourselves and be kind to our own mental and physical well being. Give yourself time to breathe. Stop pushing your mental and emotional limits all the time! Remember that self care means keeping yourself healthy, active and responsive to all of the changes in your body, mind and the world around you. Eat good food, diet if you have allowed your health to be negatively impacted by binge eating, and always present yourself to the world in a clean and put together manner.

26 Believing in yourself!

You are your own biggest cheerleader! Believe in yourself and all things will be possible. Put away the negative I can't statements or the, I'll never be able to thoughts and replace them with I can and I wills!

#27 Seek Professional Help

When you've struggled through all of the previous tips, and you feel that there really is not hope, no matter how hard you try something always brings you down. Do not consider yourself to be a failure, because even the strongest individual will quite often need help to succeed. Don't be ashamed to find a trained professional to guide you along your journey.

Chapter 8

Finding Support Groups to help you on your recovery

CoDA or Co-dependents Anonymous

Website: www.coda.org

The hope for recovery is the first step for those seeking out help. The courage to do so arises from a deep conviction that by admitting the existence of your dysfunction you will be able to begin your journey. For those who find themselves struggling with co-dependency in their relationships or co-dependent relationships that impact them, it is highly admirable that you would consider seeking the help that a group such as CoDA can provide.

CoDA is a support group originated in the ilk of Alcoholics Anonymous to help individuals shoulder the burdens that come along with being involved in an unhealthy relationship with the aid of others who have traveled the road of co-dependency before you. The common goal is to aid one another in repairing and creating healthy relationships. The only requirement to join such a group is the desire to heal your relationship and learn the methods of recovery for both of you.

Healthy relationships radiate positive energy and provide an environment to nurture a healthy family. CoDa is a recovery group aimed at providing support, courage and help to all who seek help escaping from the suffering that surrounds co-dependent relationships. The group aims to provide emotional healing methods for personal discovery and the art of loving oneself. CoDA provides a platform for improving one's perspective on life, personal growth and development of core values. There are CoDA groups in many communities, and often finds ties to the local religious community, this does not mean that you must be a godly person to attend a meeting. All you need to attend is a desire to heal, seek comfort with like minded people and a desire to help yourself improve you situation.

The process of healing is guided by a time tested 12-Step-Program that is aimed at gaining wisdom and knowledge about the place that you occupy and how to find a way to a healthy place instead. The renewal, and healing process usually consists of meeting with a group of 5-25 people who have come together to share experiences of co-dependency. Speaking and sharing is completely one's own choice, and it is not uncommon to take this moment to make the first step of admitting your dysfunction. You will often hear others in attendance introduce themselves in a manner such as "I'm a recovering ex co-dependent/ I'm a co-dependent/ Hi, my name is Seline", or so on. The preamble and the prayer of CoDA is recited by the leader. The prayer of CoDA calls to the higher power to guide the group to light, strength, hope, wisdom, warmth, love and acceptance. In addition it is a prayer to accept things unchangeable and to have the courage to do so.

CoDA provides the basic format of the meeting online at:

http://coda.org/default/assets/File/Basic%20Meeting%20Format.pdf

It is expected that the other members will remain silent out of respect when a person is speaking. The meeting consists of each member taking turns to speak about his or her own experiences of co-dependency. For all of CoDA meetings, anyone and everyone can attend. During these meetings, people recollect any memory that they want to share, regardless of their literal relevance. As people keep on sharing their stories it is not uncommon for the other members to find inspiration to heal themselves through admitting their co-dependence, and sharing their struggles with others. The group motivates each member with a strong sense of responsibility to one another and mutual counseling.

The meeting takes place in a confidential manner, the group agrees that what goes on in the meeting and who attends is not to be shared outside of the meeting room. It is not uncommon for members to share contact information for support at times when there is no meeting available. One can decide whether to include their contact information or accept that of others. Exchanging contact information with this close-knit group provides a safety net for co-dependent to be able to reach out to a supportive friend in their most vulnerable times without judgment. The goal of these meetings is to allow each member in attendance to speak about their inner conflicts. Reading of the twelve step tradition and remedies are discussed sometimes at the opening but often at the closure of the meeting. The group permits people to not just share their experiences, but also ask questions of one another, assist each other in resolving conflicts and being there to support the other members. The aim of the meeting is to provide people with safe place in which they are given the freedom to vent out all that their subconscious is waiting for. The mission of CoDA is spiritual, not religious. New members are encouraged to keep open-minded reasons about things that are shared by the members, spiritually or not.

The group meeting closes with a final prayer called the Serenity Prayer.

12-Steps to Recovery of CoDA

1. We admit we were powerless over others, that our lives had become unmanageable.

2. We believe that there is a power greater than ourselves that can aid us in our recovery.

3. Make a decision to turn our will and our lives over to the care of God as we understood God to be.

4. Take a searching and fearless moral inventory of ourselves.

5. Admitted to God, to ourselves, and to another human being the exact nature of our wrongs.

6. Were entirely ready to have God remove all the defects of our character.

7. Humbly ask God to remove our shortcomings.

8. Make a list of all persons we had harmed and strive to make amends to them all.

9. Make direct amends to such people wherever possible except when to do so would injure them or others.

10. Continue to take personal inventory and, when we were wrong, promptly admit it.

11. Seek through prayer and meditation to improve our conscious contact with God, *as we understand God*, praying only for knowledge of God's will for us and for the power to carry that out.

12. Have a spiritual awakening as the result of these steps; we tried to carry this message to other co-dependents and to practice these principles in all our affairs.

12 Traditions of CoDA

1. Our common welfare should come first; personal recovery depends upon CoDA unity.

2. For our group purpose there is but one ultimate authority: a loving higher power as expressed to our group conscience. Our leaders are but trusted servants; they do not govern.

3. The only requirement for membership in CoDA is a desire for healthy and loving relationships.

4. Each group should remain autonomous except in matters affecting other groups or CoDA as a whole.

5. Each group has but one primary purpose: to carry its message to other co-dependents who still suffer.

6. A CoDA group ought never endorse, finance, or lend the CoDA name to any related facility or outside enterprise, lest problems of money, property, and prestige divert us from our primary spiritual aim.

7. Every CoDA group ought to be fully self-supporting, declining outside contributions.

8. Co-Dependents Anonymous should remain forever nonprofessional, but our service centers may employ special workers.

9. CoDA, as such, may create service boards or committees directly responsible to those they serve.

10. CoDA has no opinion on outside issues; hence, the CoDA name ought never to be drawn into public controversy.

11. Our public relations policy is based on attraction rather than promotion; we need always to maintain personal anonymity at the level of press, radio, and films.

12. Anonymity is the spiritual foundation of all our traditions; ever reminding us to place principles before personalities.

12 Promises of CoDA

1) I know a new sense of belonging. The feelings of emptiness and loneliness will disappear.
2) I am no longer controlled by my fears. I overcome my fears and act with courage, integrity, and dignity.
3) I know a new freedom.
4) I release myself from worry, guilt, and regret about my past and present. I am aware enough not to repeat it.
5) I know a new love and acceptance of myself and others. I feel genuinely lovable, loving and loved.
6) I learn to see myself as equal to others. My new and renewed relationships are all with equal partners.
7) I am capable of developing and maintaining healthy and loving relationships. The need to control and manipulate others will disappear as I learn to trust those who are trustworthy.
8) I learn that it is possible for me to mend--to become more loving, intimate, and supportive. I have the choice of communicating with my family in a way which is safe for me and respectful of them.
9) I acknowledge that I am a unique and precious creation.
10) I no longer need to rely solely on others to provide my sense of worth.
11) I trust the guidance I receive from my Higher Power and come to believe in my own capabilities.

12) I gradually experience serenity, strength, and spiritual growth in my daily life.

Chapter 9

Resolving Issues of Self Help: Breaking Free of Depression and Inferiority Complexes

The forced manner in which we alter ourselves via co-dependency tends to be the ultimate reason for our desire to escape from codependency. The pressure to conform arises from societal pressure, childhood expectations, perceived failures and guilt experienced.

When a person applies his mind too helping himself, it is necessary to resolve the practical conflicts that arise along the way to recovery and self-help.

For example, if you've just recently broken away from your co-dependent relationship, just like all other addictions dictate, there can be withdrawal symptoms. When you start to feel this void created by the absence of your partner, feelings of depression are not uncommon. All of us prefer warmth, to isolation. There may be instances when you crave the relationship you once had and end up convincing yourself that you are unable to change and should merely return to the one you once loved. Another thing to consider is the guilt you will feel over leaving your partner stranded when you make the decision to walk away from co-dependency. This is the guilt that you have put upon yourself while it will be a struggle you must not allow it to rule you decision making. Do not allow yourself to be swayed by the good memories to forget the negative and abusive relationship you have escaped.

How to Break-free from Guilt and Depression

Resentment, regret and guilt are some of the most common factors responsible for the onset of depression, according to many studies today. Guilt is perhaps the most detrimental emotion when is comes to depression, it will take over and stick with you until that does not leave you until you consciously decide to do something about it.

Just like all blips and beeps created by the variety gadgets we own today, our body sends out regular signals in the form of dissatisfaction, guilt, resentment and stress. Each of which is a highly powerful and damaging emotion we must address in order to escape from depression. When we end up going against our own values, principles and ideologies, our subconscious sends out a signal of displeasure and often times of guilt.

The following are some of the primary steps to get over your guilt. They are:

1. Find out your most important values, ideologies, and principles.
2. Seek out the reason for your guilt
3. Curb abnormal responsibility towards the suffering of others.
4. Stop allowing excessive feelings regret about failures
5. Do not allow perfectionism trigger guilt
6. Do not allow yourself to participate in the manipulation of others
7. Stop worrying about what society thinks of you
8. Stop negative self-talks
9. Stop all over-generalization
10. Avoid emotionally illogical reasoning
11. *Increase self*-respect and self-esteem
12. Set practical goals and expectations

Steps to break free from depression

The lack of companionship and all that it brings with it are some of the main reasons that depression is exasperated in dome people. Every one of us goes through recurrent willpower failures because of the current rat race in which we live. With the current level of stress increasing for the average person in ways we never expected, it is impossible for the world to be free of depression. The state of the world in and of itself with pollution, negative news reporting, and the drag of daily struggles to make ends meet creates a constant sense of negativity that we embrace exasperating depression today.

In a co-dependent relationship, certain aspects of guilt, possessiveness, jealousy and unhealthy intimacy as well as addiction towards other things can add to the depression of an individual. The following are some of the primary steps to break free depression:

1) Stop negative self-talks
2) Spend more time with the ones you love
3) Socialize with like minded individuals
4) Seek out entertainment that interests you
5) Pampering yourself
6) Eat healthy
7) Take time to help others who share in your depression
8) Explore your hobbies and interests
9) Travel and explore the world around you
10) Cultivate positivity
11) Seek help from support groups
12) Seek professional help

How to heal hyper anxiety and Inferiority Complexes

The second part of resolving issues around the healing of your subconscious from co-dependency is to prevent hyperactive anxiety after the break-up as well as regular feelings of inferiority/ worthlessness from overpowering your well being. With hyperactive anxiety comes paranoia, nightmares and panic attacks. It is very important to focus on the reasons of hyperactive anxiety in co-dependency and ways to resolve it.

Hyperactive anxiety in co-dependency arises due to the inexperience with the situation. When a long-since habituated warmth disappears suddenly, it is natural to develop withdrawal symptoms from the body as well as the mind. Most of the times, this hyper anxiety can lead to hyperventilation as well as scary panic attacks akin to waking nightmares!

Steps to resolve hyperactive anxiety include:

1) Stop stressing that you need to reach an unknown destination in order to be living successfully, because, you simply don't need to!
2) Learn patience through involving yourself in activities like cooking, travelling, and painting or writing.
3) Meditate and conduct relaxation exercises
4) Conduct breathing exercises whenever you feel that you're hyperventilating
5) Distract yourself by listening to music that you enjoy or relaxes you.
6) Chew gum
7) Seek the company of someone you call your friend
8) Drink water
9) Seek professional help

Steps to resolve Inferiority complexes of co-dependency

1. Stop comparing yourself to anyone or anything, YOU'RE UNIQUE!
2. Everyone is different and has a different sense of reality, in short, each of us lives in our own world
3. Just as your mind is unique, so is your body....unique and precious.

4. Confront the fears that haunt you the most!
5. Talk to a close friend
6. Stop all negative self-talks, we've said it time and time again, but this step is vital to you complete recovery.
7. Look out for hidden agendas
8. Involve yourself in healthy criticisms
9. Increase your self-esteem, self-respect and self-confidence
10. Seek professional help as needed

Chapter 10

Ending Co-dependency in a healthy way

After all that has been discussed in the previous chapters regarding co-dependency, one should understand that the change and transformation of unbinding oneself from co-dependency and its negativity does not start until a person begins to do something constructive with the knowledge of their situation.

Every time that we judge or label ourselves as anything, the subconscious takes note of both positivity and negativity arising. Labeling anything enforces and emphasizes all of the effects experienced both desired or undesired.

The following elaborates some of the steps to analyze, dissect and resolve co-dependency in a healthy way inclusive of ending it properly.

1. **Determine if you are Co-dependent:**

   There is co-existing, and there is co-dependence, while one is a healthy and loving relationship the other is damaging to your self and your partner. It is important to examine all aspects of your relationship for signs of co-dependency in order to curb any destructive patterns before they become full on dysfunction. As mentioned previously, determining if an individual is in a co-dependent relationship means recognizing the symptoms and knowing the steps to cope with them rather than ignoring them and allowing them to take over your life. The easiest signal to determine co-dependency is by stepping away from the relationship. This means, take a minor break away from the routine, to determine if they are indispensable to you. This helps in understanding what things you are addicted to or dependent upon, inclusive of your partner.

2. **Filter out your honest emotions:**

   The complete understanding of co-dependency is determined when one understands the roots of their own behavioral issues as well as their inner feelings and emotions. When you become capable of filtering your own emotions, the ability to understand what is good for you and what is not becomes much more fluid. This is applicable to anyone who has become accustomed the same routine over and extended amount of time. It is necessary to filter out what is functional, dysfunctional, healthy and unhealthy for each situation that happens in your life.

3. **Mindfulness:**

   One of the most complicating and even misunderstood a topic of society is mindfulness. Mindfulness is defined as concentrating on every aspect of an action. Simply put, it is to be aware or conscious of how your actions impact others. Today, mindfulness is debated as one of the most necessary things that a person needs to attain happiness, contentment and satisfaction. It is the basic acceptance and acknowledgement of everything that we do, think or plan. Briefly said, one should start living in the present, comprehending and heeding to one's inner voice, needs, hopes and aspirations overcome failures and hurdles to attain personal success. This helps in determining the right way, towards what is good and what is not.

4. **Connect with your anger:**

   It is true that your gut feelings can help a person get over certain aspects of pain, discontent, anger and fear. Only when a person connects to their own anger can they successfully understand the toxicity of the situation. When a person is intimately acquainted with their anger the energy to overcome and reclaim the self becomes a reality. In the case of co-dependency, the damage arises due to one person's lack of boundaries physically or mentally. The belief in dysfunctional behavior and relying on that dysfunctional behavior arises from the dissatisfactions one has learned. When this crosses the limit and creates the toxic environment which propagates co-dependence in a relationship anger may be all that keeps you from seeking the tools to acquire a healthy change in your relationship. When one connects to the anger, manages it in a healthy manner as well as recognizing the damage it does to the body and mind, he is successfully armed to repair his self-wroth.

5. **End things healthy way:**

   Ending co-dependency in an unhealthy way might result in a faster separation from the individual who has caused the toxicity to seep into your life however it could very well be ineffectual and cause more damage down the road. The improper handling of co-dependency can result in an individual spending their entire life jumping from one co-dependent relationship to another without ever coming to the point where they are able to fully recover and move on in a healthy and happy way. Hence, it is imperative to take care to resolve all issues and to heal your wounds properly.

The core of ending co-dependent relationships in the best healthy way is to seek out professional assistance for yourself as well as your partner. After you have successfully made yourself aware of your co-dependent situation, how it has impacted your self and your relationship you have made the first step to resolve the dysfunction of your relationship.

Co-dependency is a term frequently used alongside co-addiction, ending both requires proper knowledge, qualification and experience. Co-dependency can be directed towards a healthy end, when both the partners start to analyze their relationship and hope to recover together. The transformation starts with finding the root of toxicity that has worked its way into your relationship. When a person starts to work out the reason for their anger and discontent, their mind starts to analyze everything, with a priority being self recovery.

The ultimate motive for healing co-dependency is learning to be a happy healthy member of society. In order to do this, it is important to understand how you have come to be in this position, identify the toxicity and seek to remove it from your life. When tolerance is exceeded and the pain is felt deeply, self-realization will drive the person to improvise and resolve their co-dependent relationships in order to heal themselves.

Hence, putting an end to the co-dependent relationship should be handled with great care and concern. Analyze the situation, dissect the root cause, and seek out the guidance to heal in a healthy way.

Chapter 11

Dysfunctional relationships and Co-dependency

One of the biggest and most obvious causes of co-dependency is dysfunction within your family relationships.

Some of the basic ways to analyze the malfunction in a family is the recurrent disagreements that occur between family members. The major causes of this friction can be,

1. Feeling unloved
2. Lack of empathy
3. Lack of understanding each other
4. Lack sensitivity
5. Denial of factual events that are negatively impacting your family
6. Recurrent and violent conflicts
7. Biases
8. Controlling behaviors
9. Adultery
10. Incest
11. Intolerance of emotional expression
12. Overprotective behavior
13. Hypocrisy
14. Cruelty
15. Demoralization
16. Apathy
17. Contempt for your loved ones
18. Promiscuity
19. Gender biases
20. Scapegoat-ing
21. Miserly attitudes
22. Blameful attitudes
23. Pawning family property
24. Withholding consent
25. Obsessive compulsive behavior

Each of these aforementioned terms can be explained in great detail, but the brevity here is merely to provide a list of negative family interactions to be aware of and attempt to prevent in your own family.. There are a million reasons of discontent and other biases that lead to situations of isolation for each family member too many to go over here. Most of the impact happens to fall upon young developing children, as they are still learning what it means to be an individual of their own merit. It is our responsibility to ensure that our children are raised in such away as to allow them to become vital members of society. This is why it is so important that we recognize dysfunction not only in ourselves, or our partner but in each relationship we are a part of. Our own mental health, and self worth, is vital to ensuring that the next generation is able to continue forward in a healthy manner as well.

Chapter 12

Preventing future Co-dependency

In order to prevent a future of co-dependencies, it is important to heal yourself, even when this means breaking free from your co-dependent relationships. Saying no to a co-dependent relationship takes strength and dedication. While you focus on healing yourself from the past co-dependent relationship, you are taking the first steps towards preventing all future relationships from going down the same road, without guilt, or shame.

When one successfully embraces self-care to prevent future co-dependency, they have found the strength to heal themselves and leave negative addictive behavior behind them. Seeking out their inner self and learning that they are far from unworthy of a healthy loving relationship. When you have been down the road of co-dependency and come out the other side a happier healthier you then you have found the tools needed to share your experience and prevent it from happening to your loved ones.

The following are some of the time tested methods of preventing co-dependency in the future.

1. **Stabilizing Control issues:** One must always try to protect and guard one's ideology. In life, there will always be circumstances which provoke one to lose their temper, self-control or peace of mind which threatens their happiness in their relationships. This is inescapable when you are part of such a large world as ours. Being part of a world filled with billions of people, one has a responsibility to society, be it their local community, the nation

they live in, or the larger world they touch online. This responsibility it to maintain control over your own life and not depend on those around you to do it for you. Support one another, yes! Demand that the world cater to you because of your dysfunction, no!

This involves learning to be open to the world around you but in such a way that allows for negative behavior to roll off your shoulders rather than dragging you back into negative behaviors. Your ex might be screaming at you in the middle of the grocery store, your instinct may be to square off and scream right back at them, but a better example for the people around you, both young and old, is to walk away from the situation and not allow it to propagate further always keeping your safety in mind.

2. **Say no to vulnerable situations:** another important decision that each of us needs to remember is how our reactions as well as others can impact the mood of a situation. When extremely vulnerable topics and people pop up, our resolve needs to be to maintain a peaceful calm about us. Do not allow another person or situation to cause you discomfort, only you can control your emotions, do not give that power away. Therefore, if you find that you are in a position that may be damaging to your mental health and well being do not hesitate to leave that situation. You are not required to stay and allow others to dicated your emotional health.

3. **Keep a check on addictive circumstances and substances:** This is one of the most difficult steps to get past, as well as to implement in the long run. Even after breaking away from different addictions, one is never completely free of that addiction

and the potential to slip down that slope is always there. It is best to simply remove these temptations from your life so as not so allow them the power they once had over you.

4. **Understand the nature of healthy relationships:** Moving on is one of the toughest things we will face in our lives, quite often the situation is such that we find we do not have the time to even mourn the loss that we have suffered before having to face that backlash of the partner we have removed from our life. We all to often find that life in and of itself must go on, the bills don't stop coming, work doesn't stop building up, the house doesn't miraculously clean itself just because we are struggling with the loss of what was once the very core of our being. After the end of a unhealthy relationship, it is not uncommon for an individual to seek comfort in the arms of another, no matter that they don't really love that person. This type of rebound relationship is not healthy and in the long run can do more harm to the both of you than you imagined. Take the time you need to seek out and allow a new healthy relationship to enter your life, don't rush it. Right now your most important relationship is with yourself. When you do find yourself in a new relationship, remember to say 'no' to addictions, unwanted influences, compulsions to repeat old trends, and self loathing behaviors. A healthy relationship is not maintained solely by one person, but from both individuals equally.

5. **Be appreciative, optimistic and positive about life:** Maintaining a new relationship, is effective only when both the partners understand, appreciate and accept each other. Acceptance requires not just the current behaviors of the person in their lives, but also accepting their past mistakes as well.

Optimism should enfold newer horizons of belief in the partner, freedom to make decisions as well as inspiration to think about the relationship a new and healthy way. Taking time to understand the efforts of the partner to make the right decisions to leave a negative place in life and find their way to a new and healthy one.

6. **Respect private time and space in all relationships:** another important aspect of co-existence requires respecting everyone's right to live their life as they wish. The giving of private time and space in all relationships is important to maintaining a healthy level of communication and a strong intimate bond between the partners. Allowing each patner time to be themselves will aid them in maintaining themselves while also being a healthy functioning part of a relationship. Take care to also include private time together, to share your ideologies, intimate thoughts, and personal aspirations. If either of these are missing, you will end up in a relentless battle to find and complete yourself that will only cause distrust and discontent in your relationship with your partner as well as your self. Our subconscious needs room to move and be free to decide what is important to us. Thus, you should never compromise your private time for anything. When starting a new relationship, be careful not to spend all of your energy absorbed in your partner, ignoring your own priorities! Simply put, as we have said over and over keep your first priority as you.

7. **Regular mediation and Relaxation exercises:** Everything that we see, smell, touch and feel are stored in our subconscious all of these sensations pile up to create a clog in our conscious mind often leading to confusion, mental distress, and exasperated distraction from the world around us when we most need it. Relaxation and medication are essential for developing a well

balanced subconscious for each of us. In order to maintain calm, take a few moments when you can to close your eyes, exhale, and inhale deeply and clear you mind, relax and all your allow your body to find its center. Try doing a few minutes of meditation or deep breathing exercises everyday right after you wake and before you go to sleep, this will allow your body to release the trouble so or the day before you sleep, and cleanse your mind of any residual riff raff when you awake allowing for a fresh day to unfold in front of you.

8. **Spend time with close friends and family more often:** Being human is all about knowing existing along side billions of other individuals; as such we are exposed to a vast amount of emotional stimulus from all around us. In order to live along side all of these souls we are destined to find ones who are so like us that we come to call them friends. All to often when we are in a co-dependent relationship we cut off ties to our families and those we have called friends for years. As we break free from the snare of co-dependence it's time to revisit our social life. Go out with friends from work, take up a hobby and find groups who share your interests. Be a positive member of society by sharing your life with others, enjoy time with like minded people and be yourself naturally. The companionship of another person is comforting and often enough to remind us of our own worth as an individual who deserves to be loved and cared for.

9. **Regularly make yourself a priority:** in the long run of life, many of us forget to take care of our own physical and mental health, that over the course of time, we tend to assert that self-care is in and of itself an unnecessary act. This could not be further

from the truth, so take the time to prioritize yourself, be selfish about your needs and reward yourself each day, for being alive! Each of us put great effort into living this life; self-care is one key that can open all the locked doors to endless freedom, contentment and happiness.

Chapter 13

Radical Reboot: Discovering Peace, Contentment and Happiness through Self-care

The end of a relationship is, simply put, is one of the worst experiences that many of us will ever be faced with. In some extremes the pain of a break up can be akin to the loss felt upon the death of a loved one. When you've successfully ended co-dependent relationship, take the time you need to mourn and find peace within ourselves. Accept what is gone, and know that you have made the right choice to move towards the happiness that we all deserve.

For all of you who are wondering, worrying and fretting over how you could have handled the relationship in a better fashion, the things you could do and should not have while replaying the incidents of the relationships, there is a 2-word answer to it, STOP IT!!! Do not beat yourself up over it any longer, you could not have done anything different, it takes two to be in a co-dependent relationship. We are all human, we make mistakes and we learn from them. This is a learning experience, and you are going to find that you are a much stronger person for the road you have been down.

Soon after a break-up, it might seem to you that everything that you do, think or even dream is cause for distress. In reality, anything that you take on no matter how badly it fails you possess the strength and stamina to over come and become a stronger person for it.

During the course of a relationship, especially a co-dependent relationship one becomes habituated with the likes and dislikes of their partner. It is necessary to first move away from the triggers of the old relationship, to undergo a radical reboot that is not just favorable, but also a catalyst to empower you to reach for your own desires and dreams. Hence, learn to prioritize yourself in order to celebrate and feel alive!

Discovering Peace

1. The first step to discovering peace in your life is believing that you are capable. Every moment not just on the weekend, holidays or vacations. The very need to find this level of calm in your life requires a commitment to the belief that you deserve to be at peace with your world. Peace is not an illusion, however fleeting it has been in your past, reach for it and it will be yours cherish it and nurture it and find that your mental well-being grows into something you never imagined you were capable of.
2. Creating a specific space where you can vent out your daily woes and worries. This allows you to have a place that you can seek comfort and release the tensions of the day in a no destructive manner. This should also be a space where you instantly feel the rush of relief upon reaching it, knowing that all your baggage can be laid down and disposed of for the time being, regardless of how long you are there. It can be a corner of your room, that favorite tree-side park bench, a table on the terrace at your favorite coffee shop, or even the Kitchen itself. Anything that you associate with relief, peace and calm is enough to provide you with a place to recover from the day.
3. Create a connection between peace and every aspect of your life. It is important to put out peace and serenity as a priority, of we will wallow away in the pain and anger of a world that we see no beauty in. Only when we find peace are we able to achieve a new level of living.

Exploring Contentment

1. Socrates once said "He is richest who is content with the least, for content is the wealth of nature."

2. Gratitude for the good and positive in your life as well as the acknowledgement of the favors others do for you brings about a contented feeling. When you become thankful for everything positive in your life, gradually the contentment of knowing that you are deserving settles in.

3. Erase negativity from your life, and brush off your regrets, instead take pleasure in the things that you do, and know that you are special.

4. Let go of the past, you can't change it so do not dwell on the could've, would've and should've thoughts.

5. Live in the present.

6. Do not fuel your discontent by participating in wasteful behavior; too often we make the mistake of thinking that material things will fill a void when we are not happy with ourselves. In fact this is not true and often leads to other problems regarding addiction to spending, the thrill of new possessions and poor financial management.

7. Stop making comparisons. You are a unique individual, there is only one of you, and none other will ever be the same. Each of us is different and none of us have had the same lives experiences, do not think for a moment that you are any less than you are because you feel that someone else has had more success. They have no walked in your shoes; they have not lived your experiences. So, do not for one moment forget how precious an individual you are

8. Share your life. Fill it with happy moments even through your struggles. Let others who are going through the same type of relationship see that there is hope at the end of a long hard battle. Show that you have survived, you are a strong and independent person now and you have found contentment in your life. Be thankful for where you have been, what you have learned and share that with the world.

9. Learn all that you can and give back be sharing the knowledge you have gained. This does not mean that you should start preaching and compelling people to follow your ways, but give back to others by sharing your experience giving them hope. Be a shoulder for them to lean on and be a friend to those in need.

10. Above all, learn to celebrate your existence.

Living a new Happiness

Happiness is momentary, true. But, sadness is as well. Peace and contentment however, are not fleeting. Through peace and contentment, one can explore the freshness of each moment and its happiness in a new light. Through self-care we can learn to live in peace and contentment every day, in a short time you will find that happiness is allowed to sneak into your life more and more often. Our happiness is precious and can not be conveyed in the complete sense to another as they do not feel happiness the same as we do, everyone feels emotions differently. Do not strive to reach another persons sense of happy…you will never succeed.

Some ways to live this new happiness is through:

1. Appreciating being alive;
2. Exploring the endless beauty of Nature and the world around us

3. Grieve freely
4. Be genuine in all that you say and do
5. Pampering yourself
6. Prioritizing yourself
7. Acknowledging your mistakes
8. Stand up for what you believe in.
9. Maintaining a positive out look on life
10. Exploring peace
11. Discovering contentment
12. Appreciating happiness!

It is never easy to get over a long term or meaningful. Take the journey to recovery seriously, know that you are not alone, and that there are others out there who have been where you are. Seek out happiness by allowing for the good to come to you, love yourself, care for yourself and you will become one with the world around you. It will be a rough road but in the end you will have reached a place of peace, contentment and happiness <u>*within yourself*</u>!

Conclusion

I'm thankful for the opportunity to have been able to take this journey with you. You have taken the first steps to treating your co-dependency, it's a long journey and there may be deep wounds that need to heal. Do not rush things, let all that we have shared here sink in over the next few days. Make a plan and begin taking the steps to become whole again. You only need to believe in yourself for a brief moment and then take action, make yourself a priority and begin.

Remember that help is out there! Do not for one moment hesitate to allow yourself the release of crying, screaming, or begging for change. Hold out your hand for help and know that there are others there who will share in your journey.

Good Luck.

Highly Recommended Codependency Books:

1.

How To Live In The Present Moment: Let Go Of The Past & Stop Worrying About The Future

2. Codependent No More: How to Stop Controlling Others and Start Caring for Yourself

3. Codependency: Gone For Good - How to Stop Worrying, Stop Controlling, and Put Yourself First

4. You're Not Crazy - You're Codependent.: What Everyone Affected by Addiction, Abuse, Trauma or Toxic Shame Needs to Know

BONUS: Free Books & Special Offers

I want to thank you again for purchasing this book! I would like to give you access to a great service that will e-mail you notifications when we have FREE books available. You will have FREE access to some great titles before they get marked at the normal retail price that everyone else will pay. This is a no strings attached offer simply go to www.globalizedhealing.com to get free books

Copyright 2014 by Globalized Healing, LLC - All rights reserved.

Made in the USA
Lexington, KY
06 September 2015